# Leading
# by Example

## The Lessons Learned Series

Through the power of personal storytelling, each book in the Lessons Learned series presents the accumulated wisdom of some of the world's best known experts, and offers insights into how these individuals think, how they approach new challenges, and how they use hard-won lessons from experience to shape their leadership philosophies. Organized thematically, according to the topics at the top of managers' agendas, each book draws from Fifty Lessons' extensive video library of interviews with CEOs and other thought leaders. Here, the world's leading senior executives, academics, and business thinkers speak directly and candidly about their triumphs and defeats. Taken together, these powerful stories offer the advice you'll need to take on tomorrow's challenges.

## Other books in the series:

*Managing Change*
*Managing Your Career*

# Leading by Example

Harvard Business School Press

*Boston, Massachusetts*

Printed in the United States of America
11 10 09 08     5 4 3 2

Library of Congress Cataloging-in-Publication Data
Leading by example.
    p. cm. — (The lessons learned series)
  Lessons learned : straight talk from the world's top
business leaders
  ISBN-13: 978-1-4221-1859-7 (pbk. : alk. paper)
  1. Leadership. I. Title: Lessons learned : straight talk
from the world's top business leaders.
  HD57.7.L43744 2007
  658.4'092—dc22
                              2007019474

In partnership with Fifty Lessons, a leading provider of digital media content, Harvard Business School Press is pleased to announce the launch of Lessons Learned, a new book series that showcases the trusted voices of the world's most experienced leaders. Through the power of personal storytelling, each book in this series presents the accumulated wisdom of some of the world's best-known experts and offers insights into how these individuals think, approach new challenges, and use hard-won lessons from experience to shape their leadership philosophies. Organized thematically according to the topics at the top of managers' agendas—leadership, change management, entrepreneurship, innovation, and strategy, to name a few—each book draws from Fifty Lessons' extensive video library of interviews with CEOs and other thought leaders.

## A Note from the Publisher

Here, the world's leading senior executives, academics, and business thinkers speak directly and candidly about their triumphs and defeats. Taken together, these powerful stories offer the advice you'll need to take on tomorrow's challenges.

We invite you to join the conversation now. You'll find both new ways of looking at the world, and the tried-and-true advice you need to illuminate the path forward.

# CONTENTS

# Contents

# Leading
# by Example

# The Importance of a Visible Leader

## Will Whitehorn

*President, Virgin Galactic*

ONE OF THE IMPORTANT lessons I've gained from working for Virgin for eighteen years is that having a strong leader in a business is incredibly important and much underestimated in large, corporate organizations—somebody who's prepared to take

## Leading by Example

the heat for things and let the buck stop with him.

I remember Richard Branson being interviewed on Radio Five Live, which is a BBC radio station in the UK, several years ago. He was talking about some of the problems that Virgin Trains had had, not due to our own fault but down to something at Railtrack. We'd had a problem with a train that got stuck, but we hadn't dealt with it very effectively. He went on the radio to talk about this, and he said, "We messed up; it was completely our fault; I take full responsibility for it. We're obviously looking at not doing it again in the future, but there's no point in hiding from the fact that we've got to do this better if we're going to make this business work."

Now, a lot of business leaders wouldn't do that. They would come on the radio, for instance, or a television program, and they'd try and blame something in the organization, but before that they'd try and blame the outside world for their own issues. So I think people have more to fear from not having strong leadership in an organization than from having it, because strong leaders tend to take decisions. Again, I think one of the important lessons of business is that it is better to take a decision that may turn out to be wrong and that you might have to change than to take no decision at all and drift in limbo.

What we try to do at Virgin is to create strong leaders in the organization. They are all people who are given a sense of responsibility; the buck stops with them, and they've got to get on with what they're doing—and they are free to do so. As long as they meet the business plan—the criteria, the parameters, and the amount of money they've got to spend—they're given a lot of freedom, and we also give them freedom to build their profile.

For instance, in Australia you'll find as many Australians have heard of the guy who runs the airline there, Brett Godfrey, as have heard of Richard Branson because Brett has the profile there. We have deliberately, he has deliberately, and Richard has deliberately tried to push him to build that profile because he has to deal with the problems that the Australian business has had over the years.

The more profile you have as a business leader in a marketplace, the more chance you have of getting issues over to the public when they come about.

✦

# TAKEAWAYS

- ⚐ It is critical in business to have strong leaders who are prepared to take responsibility for the organization's actions and let the buck stop with them.

- ⚐ People have more to fear from *not* having strong leadership in an organization; strong leaders tend to make decisions when everyone else shies away from them.

## Leading by Example

⚔ The more visibility business leaders
   have in a marketplace, the more chance
   they have of explaining issues to the
   public when they inevitably occur.

# Setting the Right Tone at the Top

## Sir Michael Rake

*Chairman, KPMG International*

IN THE LAST three or four years, we look at what's happened in the business world, and there's been a complete breakdown in trust.

There's been a complete breakdown in trust in the operation of the capital markets and a complete breakdown in trust of chief executives and the way they operate. The assumption has been that everyone operates out of a sense of greed, if not dishonesty—to enrich themselves at the expense of others. This is what's happened as a result of all the corporate scandals that we've seen, not only in the United States—actually we saw it in the UK a few years ago too.

Of course, as a result of that, we've seen an enormous amount of regulation, legislation, litigation, and rule making. The reason we've had these problems—this lack of trust and these cases of extreme behavior and extreme greed—is actually because of the culture of the organization, in my view. I've seen it in many companies we've investigated. Yes, things can go wrong from a control and environmental point of view; but if you come down to the culture, how often you see that it's the tone at the top—the tone that an individual leader sets—that is incredibly important to the way the whole organization works.

One of the things that we all need to understand when we take responsibility for public companies—whether we're advisers to them, auditors to them, or nonexecutive directors in them—is how important this issue is. Because if you don't have the right tone, or the right culture, it's amazing how even intelligent people will somehow become overwhelmed by that tone or culture. Clearly that's the case in Enron and the case in many other companies that you've seen, where the culture went wrong at the top.

I think this leads into real leadership by example, because one of the key things leaders have to understand is that they're very visible. Anything they do is really exaggerated in the communication of any company, so their attitude toward "living what they say" is very important, as is their attitude toward the basic values. How do people behave with each other? What is the sense of integrity? What is the sense of respect for people within the organization, whatever their level; do they have real respect for them—not just have a charter? Enron had an enormously laudable charter of values in corporate social responsibility, but actually it was almost a smokescreen for abuse.

## Leading by Example

What you need to have is people seeing that it isn't a charter of values or corporate social responsibility; it's actually meant to be the way that people at the top really behave—to live the values of the organization. Corporate social responsibility is not only the right thing to do in the communities in which we operate, but the business case is enormously important: it adds value to your brand, it adds prestige and pride to your people, it aids recruitment and retention, and it also creates the right culture within a capitalist world.

The only reason we have capitalism and public companies is to create wealth for many, not just a few. Trust in organizations has to be seen and believed by employees, regulators, politicians, and journalists. The company has to act it out; it has to really deliver and live it—and that always starts, in my experience, with the example of the guy or the lady at the top.

In investigations we've done into companies and individuals where things have gone wrong, what's stunning is that very often you find people within an organization where the culture's wrong, or the tone at the top is wrong, that have crossed from white, to gray, to black. Most of them have to operate in the gray a lot of the time, and often when they cross into the black and they've committed an illegal act—actually criminal—they haven't realized it. When you talk to them and interview them, you find that because the culture of the organization's gone wrong—the tone at the top is wrong—and because of the aggressiveness with which the targets are set or the way in which their achievement of those targets is rewarded, intelligent, honest people suddenly think that this act is okay: because within that environment it seems to be okay. It isn't okay; they've actually done something which is illegal or amoral.

You have to create an approach that actually rewards the right culture. You have to have some role models: people who are promoted who are seen to be those who demonstrate these values, that integrity, and that approach to others. You have to be seen to frankly deal with people who, having been properly counseled or advised, still do not adopt those values. However clever they might be, however technically brilliant they might be, if they're creating an environment where the culture is wrong, then they're going to be a net deficit to the organization, and you need to seriously think about removing them. It's like a cancer: it creates an environment where people think that's the way you have to be in order to survive or to succeed, and that's very damaging for an organization.

I'm not saying, obviously, that every case ends like Enron; but you see a lot of companies that fail and become inefficient, where people become unmotivated, and it's hard work. In a large organization you have to work very hard at ensuring people understand these values and the way they should operate. I think that the basic lesson here is the huge responsibility on any leader to set the right tone at the top, to live the values the company espouses, and to really lead by example.

---

# TAKEAWAYS

---

- It is the leader's responsibility to set the right tone, live the values the company espouses, and truly lead by example.

- A leader must deal decisively with people who do not adopt corporate values, as they are a net deficit to an organization. Leaders must promote the right culture by promoting/rewarding those who lead by example and demonstrate the corporate tone.

- Leaders should become more "visible": they should attend lower-level meetings and set an example by talking about the importance of CSR and by setting the right tone for the company.

# Leadership 24/7

## Ken Freeman

*Managing Director, KKR*

I'D BEEN RUNNING Quest Diagnostics for about two or three years, and we were in the middle of our turnaround. We were starting to see, ever so slightly, some gradual improvement in our business. And I was on vacation, the first vacation I'd taken in eons, with my family—my wife and our daughter and our son. We had gone to Orlando to spend some time in Central Florida for a

spring break. We were heading to the airport, got to the airport a little bit early,
went through the gates for security, and
were walking down toward our specific gate
for our flight back to the New York area.
All of a sudden, an individual came running up to me, and he said, "You're Ken
Freeman."

Now, you can imagine my fifteen-year-
old daughter and my twelve-year-old son
were kind of inspired—Gee, Dad, here's
somebody in the middle of Orlando airport
coming up to you and saying "You're Ken
Freeman." And I kind of girded myself and
said, "Yes, I am."

As things moved on, as we discussed
things, he said, "Look, I want to introduce
myself. You met me about a month ago
here in Florida. I was over in Tampa at one
of the big labs we have, and I'm a courier
for Quest Diagnostics. I just want you to
know, Ken, that I've met you once, and I've
attended a town meeting personally, and I
come to the virtual town meetings where we
see you and hear from you and hear your

voice mails. I just wanted you to know that I
am in your corner. We are going to turn
this company around. We're going to become a great company, and your leadership
is going to get us there. I'm going to be one
of those folks on the ground that's going to
make it happen. Ken, I'd like you to meet
my family."

I introduced my family to his family; we
became fast friends; we chatted for five or
ten minutes. In the end, we parted good
friends, and—even more importantly, I
think—my kids were inspired. They said,
"Gee, Dad, is this how business really
works?" And I said, "Well, kids, it can work
a lot of different ways. But there's a lesson
from this encounter we've had, this chance
encounter in the middle of nowhere. I
could've reacted to this guy and said, 'Well,
who are you? I don't want to talk to you. I'm
here with my family. I'm on vacation. I want
to be with my family in an airport as op-
posed to dealing with being nice to an employee and engaging in a constructive way.'
And what do we see?"

# Leading by Example

And my family said, "Well, what we saw was an interaction of two people who really seemed to get along." And I said, "That's the issue." The lesson of leadership for here is really very simple, and that is, as leaders and as individuals, we have to be who we are twenty-four hours a day, seven days a week.

The informal interactions are as important—and I would argue even more important—in leadership than the formal, structured, canned interactions that happen so often day in and day out in our business lives. That informal interaction really is how somebody will form their opinion of you. People want their leaders to be human beings above all else.

They hear so many of us talk about values and behaviors, and what it takes to make our company strong. If we don't exhibit those behaviors in those informal settings—if I'd been yelling at my family or we'd been having an altercation of some sort, as so often happens in airports all over this country—

## Leading by Example

how would that employee have reacted? He would have said, "He doesn't walk the talk of the values he keeps talking about."

The most exciting part of a situation like the Orlando incident is, the courier didn't keep quiet about it. He went back and told his colleagues back in the Tampa laboratory, "You know, I met Ken and his family at the airport. They're all nice people, and they really are committed to helping us turn around our company. And I told him I'm committed, too. And we can't let Ken down; we can't let our business down." And it spread through the couriers' department; it spread beyond that into the overall laboratory in Tampa, Florida.

So even when we think a chance getting together with somebody might not have any value at all, the end result is, every moment of every day, our leadership shines through, good or bad; and whatever shines through, good or bad, is going to get communicated beyond the little circle where the actual dialogue took place.

---

# TAKEAWAYS

---

- ⚔ Chance encounters can offer leaders special opportunities to reinforce their behaviors and belief systems. Individuals form their opinions of leaders through informal interactions; they want their leaders to be human above all else.

- ⚔ Leaders must display consistent behaviors and leadership skills in both personal and professional interactions twenty-four hours a day, seven days a week.

- ⚔ Leaders must be aware that much value exists in informal communication, which allows leadership skills—good or bad—to show through.

—◆◆◆—

# The Front Line Is the Bottom Line

—◆◆◆—

## Julia Cleverdon

*Chief Executive Officer,
Business in the Community*

WHEN I STARTED my working life at British Leyland's Swindon body and assembly plant, I realized early on that the front line is the bottom line. What matters most is

**Leading by Example**

what the front line understands about the issues; the challenges; and the need for flexibility, accuracy, efficiency, and producing the goods you said you were going to produce at the time you said you would. In my career and in working with companies, I'm always fascinated about whether we recognize that the front line is the bottom line.

Starting as a very junior industrial relations officer in a car plant just outside Swindon that employed twenty-seven thousand people on one site, with thirty-two different trade unions, I had the most junior job in the place. There was nobody more junior than me—other than the industrial relations department's cat.

I carried the negotiations notebooks for the shop stewards into the meetings in the morning, and I stamped the time-keeping cards in the afternoon. I realized after six months of stamping these cards that actually there were more people sick under Smith than under Brown. And if you moved Smith, the lot that were well got sick, and the lot that were sick got well. The team

## Leading by Example

leader responsible and accountable for achieving results on the front line is the single most important character responsible for whether you are going to achieve or not.

So whenever consultants say to me, "It's very important who's at the top; it sets the whole tone," I always think, "Actually, the most important person is the highest-level one who knows the front line." That's the hinge where you make things happen.

I realized that the front line was the bottom line when I was working for The Industrial Society. Nobody ever believes this happened to me, but it did. I came back on a train late at night and missed the train I was meant to catch on into London. I was at Peterborough station at about one o'clock in the morning, waiting for the milk train to go through at three. The only thing to watch was the nightly pantomime that goes on at every single train station in Britain, or used to then: the sorting of the mail.

British Rail stood on the train, and Royal Mail stood on the platform. British Rail threw the bags out into trucks, and Royal

## Leading by Example

Mail took the decision which truck they were to go into. I was watching it, as I've always been fascinated by what happens with decision making—not at the board level but at the front line.

The conversation highlighted that they were sorting to go either west to Wales or north to Scotland. As they shouted out where the bag was to go, Royal Mail took the decision. And the conversation went: "Aberdare"—"Aberdare"; "Abersoch"—"Abersoch"; "Aberaeron"—"Aberaeron"; "Aberystwyth"—"Aberystwyth"; "Aberdare"—"Aberdare"; "Aberdeen"—"Aberdeen"; "Abersoch"—"Abersoch." Every single bag went straight off into the Welsh truck.

I leaned forward and said, "I'm frightfully sorry to get in the way, but I think that Aberdeen is in Scotland, and I suspect that that bag should have gone in the Scottish truck, not the Welsh one." And the two representatives of these two mighty great organizations spun on their heels, looked at me, and said, "Are you trying to teach us how to do our jobs?"

I said, "No, no way; I'm just terribly sorry for all the people who put a first-class stamp on the letter in the hope that he got the birthday card in the morning, or he got the letter that said, 'I'm sorry what I said on the phone, darling, it's very easy to be difficult on the phone,' or the income tax return that would arrive one day earlier to save the overdraft. Because that's what it's about: accuracy and efficiency, and producing the goods you said you were going to produce, at the time you said would." They looked at me with pity and wouldn't move the bag.

That picture remains with me forever about how you get people at the front line to care about what they do and how they do it. For me, that's been a driving passion about the importance of communication and consultation. By and large, the front line knows exactly what we ought to do—it's just that nobody's bothered to ask them much.

# Leading by Example

I've always said—and it drives everybody mad in my office—that paper is patient; the paper will still be there, but the people will have gone. You have to seize this one moment to catch a sales team coming back from a successful pitch or, even more important, to catch them coming back from an unsuccessful pitch. You've got to be with people on the issues and the deals in that moment, not sitting in offices studying the computer returns, which by and large measure yesterday's failure rather than tomorrow's opportunities.

So work alongside people. Walk the job; have it in the diary. Walk the job in those bits of the office that are farthest away from where you normally go to the loo; get a cup of coffee and walk out from reception. Try to understand what it feels like: Are we clear about customers? Do we know what we're doing? Have we won?

For me, the front line is the bottom line. The leadership at the front line, and the support of that leadership, is the single most important thing that any manager or leader can do.

# TAKEAWAYS

- ⚐ Leadership of the front line is the most important facet of a manager's job. The front line often knows exactly what needs to be done, but often nobody bothers to ask them.

- ⚐ Leaders should visit all parts of the office, not just those that they pass through regularly.

- ⚐ Team leaders and their attitudes are pivotal to achievement. They should celebrate and commiserate with staff, be with them, and understand their issues.

# Be a Servant Leader

## William Pollard

*Chairman Emeritus, ServiceMaster*

THE FIRST TIME I was confronted with a lesson of servant leadership was when I was recruited to join ServiceMaster. I'd practiced law for ten years and had served in the administration on the faculty of Wheaton College right here in Wheaton, Illinois. I was ready to go back to the practice of law when I was recruited to join ServiceMaster.

## Leading by Example

Ken Hansen and Ken Wessner were participating in the recruiting. Ken Hansen was the chairman; Ken Wessner was the president of the company. They were both great salespeople. At that time, ServiceMaster was a small public company. They created a great picture of what it could be, and in the process of painting the picture in the recruiting process, they implied many times that maybe some day, I might be able to lead this company.

So I decided, that last day of the interview, that I would press them because I was going to give up the opportunity of going back to a law firm to come here to a new environment, and I needed to know what I needed to get done in order to become president and CEO of this company. How long would it take, what were the obstacles, and what was the competition? I just wanted to assess the whole situation before I said yes.

Well, I started to press Ken Hansen, and after about five minutes he looked at me in the eye and said, "Bill, the interview is over." And Ken Wessner ushered me to the

# Leading by Example

front door of ServiceMaster. And I left ServiceMaster, and I said, "I guess I've blown
this opportunity, and I'm going back to
practice law."

Two days later, Ken Hansen called me
up, and he said, "Bill, do you want to understand what happened in my office the
other day?" and I said, "Sure!"

He said, "Will you have breakfast with me
tomorrow morning?" And we did. At that
breakfast meeting, he said, "Bill, if you want
to come and contribute, you'll have a great
opportunity; but if you're coming for a title
or a position, forget it."

And then he launched into a discussion
on what it meant to be a servant leader in
ServiceMaster. I learned some lessons:
never give a title or a position to someone
who can't live without it; always be willing to
walk in the shoes of those you lead; and
never ask somebody to do something that
you're not willing to do yourself.

And Ken, in his own way, tested me. The
first eight weeks of my time at ServiceMaster
was not spent in my role as a senior officer

but out doing the service work that our service workers did every day. I had many experiences during that time, reminding me of
the importance of those service people; my
reliance upon them. And little did I realize
when I was doing that work, that some day it
would involve over two hundred thousand
people that we either managed or employed
in doing service work.

Servant leadership was a learning experience for me, and it was a continuing learning experience for me. One of the things
that happens typically in organizational behavior is that as your responsibilities grow,
so do the trappings of office. And often the
trappings of office—whether it's a corner
office literally, whether it's the size of car
you drive, or whether you get a parking
space, or whatever it is—keep removing you
from the people whom you're leading and
whom you're responsible for.

One of the ways in ServiceMaster that we
kept reminding ourselves of the importance
of being willing to serve was by initiating a

## Leading by Example

"We Serve" day. And so everyone in the company at least once a year had the responsibility to go out and deliver one of our services. It didn't make any difference whether you were a senior officer, whether you were working in the accounting department, or whether you were working in information technology; whatever your job was in the company, part of your job was to go out and deliver our service.

———•••———

# TAKEAWAYS

———•••———

- ⚑ Servant leadership is a continuous learning process, and its values must be instilled in every member of the organization.

- ⚑ As leaders get farther away from the in-the-trenches responsibilities, it's

## Leading by Example

easy for them to become removed
from the people for whom they are
responsible.

⚐ Leaders should always be willing to
walk in the shoes of those they lead and
should never ask anyone to do something they would be unwilling to do
themselves.

# The Head Gardener

## Lord Sharman

*Chairman, Aegis Group*

YOU MUST FOCUS on the strengths of an individual—what they're good at rather than what they're not so good at. The reason I say that is because you can't build on a weakness. A weakness is there: it's something you have to take into account, but the way in which you get superior performance out of a group of people is to figure out

what they're good at and then get them
into a role that uses that to the maximum
advantage.

I'm very fond of gardening myself, and
I'm fond of gardening examples. To some
degree, developing people in an organization is impossible. You can't develop them;
they develop themselves, and so your job is
like that of a head gardener. You figure out
what the various microclimates are around
the place, and then you figure out the quali-
ties of the plants that you need to go into
those microclimates. Similarly, you select
the people based on their strengths and
place them in those jobs. I've seen notes of
appraisal interviews, which say that two-
thirds of the interview is spent talking about
what the guy's not good at. Now, that's
great—I can't imagine anybody coming out
of an interview like that feeling anything
other than very depressed.

What you want to do is spend time talking
about what the person is good at and how
he's going to develop that. Sure, see whether
you can do something about the weaknesses,

but to my way of thinking, appraisal interviews should be two-thirds about what the person is good at and how those great assets can be used within the organization. If you look at good coaches in the sports field—and I've always been fascinated about how good coaches work—they don't actually coach technique very often. The really good coaches are the ones that coach the mind and the attitude.

You'll always have people who find it much easier to be critical than to be encouraging. The tone at the top has to be right. If you start criticizing your colleagues about what they're bad at all the time rather than encouraging them, that's sure as hell going to get down through the organization very quickly.

When I was at KPMG, I insisted that one of the senior guys meet every person joining the organization. It didn't matter whether he or she was a typist, telephonist, graduate recruit, or somebody being brought in as a senior manager; the induction programs were always attended by people at the top level of the organization. I used to do half a dozen a year myself.

In some organizations, sponsorship is extremely strong and extremely important, and there's the notion that you're not going to get anywhere unless you work for a sponsor—that you have to go and work for him or her to get on. I don't think that's desirable, but I do think having someone who takes an interest in you and helps you over the bad times, as well encouraging you through the good is very important—particularly to young individuals and in retaining people.

With people-based industries, every time you lose somebody you're losing an investment. People don't like me saying this, but it's like writing off a piece of new plant. If you had to write off a production facility because it was no longer useful to you, people would get quite exercised about the impact on the accounts. If you lose ten guys or girls whom you've spent the last five years developing, that's as big an investment; it just doesn't show up on the balance sheet.

# TAKEAWAYS

- Leaders must focus on the strengths of individuals and how their assets can be used within the organization.

- In people-based industries, every time a leader loses a member of staff they have trained and nurtured over the years, they are losing an investment.

- Performance appraisals should be two-thirds about the positives. If leaders start criticizing their people rather than encouraging them, it will soon spread to the rest of the staff and reflect negatively on leadership in the company.

——◀●▶——

# Listening at All Levels

——◀●▶——

## Dawn Airey

*Former Managing Director,*
*Sky Networks, BSkyB*

IF YOU RUN AN ORGANIZATION, it's absolutely critical to listen to everybody at every level—not only to get a sense of what is going on, but also to understand the issues and the dynamics of an organization.

About ten years ago, I was in charge of children's programs for ITV. I was coming

## Leading by Example

across from Central Television, where I was director of broadcasting. My first day on the job was like the post office letters to Father Christmas. There were sacks and sacks and sacks of proposals.

I thought, "How do we go through all of this?" So my PA, Elspeth, and I literally just burned the midnight oil to get through them. To be frank, you can read from the first page whether it's good or bad, and we invariably had to take some pretty visceral decisions—yes, yes, no, yes, no. We got through it all with a certain amount of speed and were very, very ruthless.

As I said, you could tell straight away whether something was going to work or not. If something was going to work and you wanted to get the production company in, you'd say, "That's a number-one response, so get them in the diary; we'll get them in and talk to them."

Number two would be—and this was very rare—a, "Maybe, but I just need a bit more information," or "I just need to see how the schedule pans out."

# Leading by Example

Number three—the second-best answer in broadcasting—is a swift "No."

A number four would also be a swift "No," but it would be a swift no with respect, so we would send it out seven days on. If it came from a very well-known production company or one of the ITV companies, you wouldn't turn around and say "No" immediately because they'd think, "Oh, you haven't considered it"—whereas you had considered it, and you knew. But you didn't say that to the companies because they would get really upset if they got a rejection the next day. So it would be a number four; which was a polite turn down, but we'll send the letter in seven days.

And so one of the shows came from an independent, and it was about St. Tiggy-winkle's, which is a little wildlife hospital in Buckinghamshire. I said, "Elspeth, that's definitely a number four," and she said, "Oh, I rather like that idea." I said, "Well I don't really care whether you rather like the idea or not. I don't, and I'm the controller of kids' programs. Number four."

So, about a week later, we were doing a review, which I always do at the end of each week to see what's outstanding and what letters we have sent out, just recap and see if there are any patterns in terms of what's going on.

I said, "That number four hasn't gone out yet—the St. Tiggywinkle's. It should have gone out." Elspeth said, "Well, I'm not going to send it. I don't think it should be a number four. I think they should come in and talk to you because I think it's a really good idea." I said, a bit cheeky, "Just go back to making the coffee and typing up." And she replied, "Nope. I'm going to ask them to come in." I looked at her: "Give me that proposal again." So I read it, and I still didn't quite get it—quite cutesy, with little hedgehogs with their arms in plaster and all that— very sweet, but . . . But I said, "All right, then." She had just kept banging on about it.

So we got the company in, and actually it was a nice idea. I thought, "Well, if she's really passionate about it, maybe she's right; maybe we should commission it." We did, and it did spectacularly well.

Now this is a lesson in listening to a voice that is employed to do one thing, but actually is very bright and can input into what you're doing and just occasionally say, "You don't have all the answers, and I think you should rethink what you're doing." And she was absolutely right. You *do* have to listen to those people around you and just sometimes stand back and say, "Yes, actually you should have the chance to do this."

I now operate a system with my key creatives. As I said, I have twenty years' experience in television, so I like to think I know what I'm doing most of the time. But programming is not an exact science.

So I give all of my key creatives two cards, which they're allowed to play at any point because these are imaginative cards. They can come along and say, "This is something I know you are not going to like. In fact, I know you're going to hate it. But I really love it and want to do it, and I'm going to play that card." And nobody has ever let me down. They've always been right.

So you give what are not quite "get out of jail" cards but "something that you really want to do that I can't question, because you're employed as a senior creative" cards. I'm employed to give guidance and strategic direction and to try to give the benefit of my experience. But my experience is different from somebody else's. And you can't be dogmatic; you can't say you have the answers all the time. You say, "OK—play your card. If you play it and you're right, you get two cards back." And it works.

---

# TAKEAWAYS

---

◁  Leaders should realize that listening to people at every level within the organization is crucial, both to get a sense of the internal dynamics but also to pick up on good ideas.

> As difficult as it may be, leaders must accept that sometimes they do not know best. Other people have ideas that are valuable to the organization and from which they should learn. Sometimes the best ideas come from people who haven't actually been employed for their expertise in that area.

> Leaders should foster an environment that encourages people to contribute their ideas. They should hold meetings with direct reports and ask them directly if they have any ideas they want to share.

# Leadership Is Not a Popularity Contest

## Sanjiv Ahuja

*Chief Executive, Orange Group*

THERE IS A BIG MYTH in business that you need a buy-in of your strategy from your team, and also I think there's a big myth believed by leaders that they need to win the popularity contest inside a company.

## Leading by Example

As a leader of a business, be very clear in your mind that you are not running a democracy. By virtue of the fact that you have been anointed the leader, there is a significant degree of autocracy that comes with you. When you make decisions and when you make choices, they're not always the most popular.

If your objective was to ensure that your team bought into your strategy and liked what you did, then, candidly, you are not needed as a leader. You could do a continuous poll and determine what decisions and direction the company ought to take, do it from morning until night, and then everybody votes on it—and the business goes wherever.

You, as a leader, are supposed to make some decisions that are necessarily not going to be very popular. And that is OK; but stand up and be counted for those decisions. Sometimes those decisions are where you bet your job, but that's OK; stand up and be counted for those. Look at the history of mankind—all successful leaders at different stages of their lives have made those decisions. In our efforts, these are "bet your job" decisions, and that's OK; other people have "bet your life" decisions. Many successful leaders have made "bet your life" decisions successfully, and some unsuccessfully.

Some of us make decisions successfully, some unsuccessfully, but most of the decisions we make are not that critical. But we must make decisions, and you must not get deluded with the absolute myth that you need to be a popular leader.

You need to be an *effective* leader; you need to be a *decisive* leader. And while you are leading with effectiveness, decisiveness, clarity, and the passion for the success of your business, your team eventually does follow you.

I'll give you an example. Ten years ago I was brought into a business where employee morale was down, product quality was down, the profits were in a terrible shape, and the revenue was in decline for many years. Most of the customers thought that it wasn't a business that could be turned around; most of the employees thought it wasn't a business that could be turned around either.

When I stepped in, I did have to make a significant number of changes. I changed most of the leadership team, I changed a good part of the management team that worked for those leaders, and essentially I restructured the business. In the early days I probably wasn't the most popular leader. Actually, I *know* I was not the most popular leader. But by the time we had finished the transformation, the company was delivering world-class performance in the area it was engaged in, in terms of quality, delivery, productivity, profitability, and growth. In all criteria, it was performing in a world-class manner, and I would like to say that by the time I left I was probably the most popular leader that company had ever had. But if I were looking at employee polls, I probably wouldn't have taken any of the tough decisions that I had to take.

Like all leaders in all situations, you have to make the tough calls—but stand up for those and be counted. Don't shy away, and don't get confused between popularity and the right choices. Right choices and popularity do not have to go hand in hand.

---

# TAKEAWAYS

---

⊣ A leader does not run a democracy. Leaders must make the tough decisions necessary to benefit the company's profitability and performance, not their own popularity.

⊣ The toughest decisions will sometimes be the most unpopular ones. If leaders need to make unpopular choices, they should call a meeting and explain to people why the decisions are necessary.

⚏ If staff members have grievances, leaders should ask them to voice their concerns. A leader may need to talk through why particular concerns are not in the best interests of the company.

# Use Emotion Sparingly

## David Michels

*Former Group Chief Executive, Hilton Group*

EMOTION IS A VALUABLE TOOL in business, but it has to be used very sparingly. I use emotion—and can use enormous emotion—whether it's anger or fear or anything else. But to do this you can only get excited so many times a year; and when you do, then everything has to quake. Try it once a week, and everyone's going to ignore you.

## Leading by Example

But there are occasions, particularly when there are people around who don't know you, when emotion can really work.

There's one example I remember when I was on the board of Arcadia, sold two or three years ago to Phillip Green. It was a board that had to decide whether to sell the company for a price vastly higher than it had been when most of us had started. Stuart Rose, currently of Marks & Spencer fame, was the chief executive who had been brought in to save the company.

I was simply a nonexecutive, and we had a great chairman, Adam Broadbent, but at the end of the day we still had to sit there with the responsibility of deciding, "Do we sell it on? Are we doing the right thing for the shareholders?" And you can't take a straw poll.

I wouldn't say it was near the cut; we were fairly certain we were right, but in the middle of the meeting, Stuart Rose stood up and said, "I can get us an extra dividend." Now, an extra dividend was 7 or 8p added onto the share price. But he didn't say it in that tone of voice; he said, "I CAN GET

# Leading by Example

IT!" And it obviously became an emotional challenge.

Now I admired Stuart enormously, but he was due to get an enormous amount of money anyhow. But he said, "I can go to Phillip Green, I can talk him through it, and I can get that extra 7p," multiplied by however tens of million shares it was. We were all a bit doubtful because it was definitely an emotional outburst rather than a fine money calculation. Off went Stuart. We all came back about six hours later, and Stuart came back with his 7p.

I wasn't there; I didn't see the conversation. They're both hard men, but I'm absolutely sure it was not a scientific agreement based on the value because there was no possibility of a scientific agreement; we'd more or less reached that decision already. It was an emotional "I have to have this sort of deal, or it won't be done" response and obviously, or willingly—we'll never know—Phillip Green was prepared to buy that. You'd never have done it by letter; you'd never have done it by calculator. You can only do it with real emotion.

## Leading by Example

I remember trying to inspire one hundred general managers to stick by a brand name that was not yet famous—the hotel chain Stakis. I would never do it again—and I'd never done it before—but I quoted Martin Luther King Jr. I won't give you the quote—because everybody knows it—but genuinely, without planning, I managed to have tears in my eyes because I really cared. This is not something that you can rehearse unless you're a full-time actor, and I'm not. I'm trying to be a full-time businessman— and that takes enough time. But I really did care; they knew I cared, and it ricocheted around the room. On that occasion it was pure, pure emotion. I managed to transfer it from the platform to the audience and back again, which inspired me more. When you can get that degree of electricity purely from emotion, it works.

Emotion is a tool you bring out the toolbox only very, very rarely; and it's something that comes by instinct. It's not something that you plan for or something that should be part of your upfront arsenal. It's just something that's there; something in your brain ticks and says, "Oh, use the emotional card." But it's the joker in the pack; it's a card you play once every fifty-two times.

━━━ ◆◆◆ ━━━

# TAKEAWAYS

━━━ ◆◆◆ ━━━

- Emotion is a valuable tool in business, but it has to be treated sparingly. Leaders should trust their gut instincts about when to use emotion—it's not always something they can plan for.

- When leaders feel themselves getting emotional in business dealings, they should pause for a few seconds to take a couple of deep breaths and ask, "Is this really the right time to use the emotional card?" They should wait until the emotion has subsided so that the conversation is less highly charged.

# The Humble Boss

## Lord MacLaurin

*Former Chairman and CEO, Tesco*

ONE OF THE LESSONS I learned very early on—which is so, so right—is that the humblest person in the organization is the most important. Never, ever forget that.

If you're going into a store and you go to the back door man and chat to him, or to the cleaner, they can go home and say, "Do you know, the chairman was in today, and he was asking me how the family were and was chatting to me." They feel good about it.

It's all about man management and getting close to people, not having an arrogant attitude that you can walk into the store and think you're God's gift to retailing.

Nobody's that, whatever business you're in; whether you look at my experiences in Tesco or my recent experiences in Vodafone. I've always said to all my people, wherever I have been, that you should chat to people and ask them how they are. At the end of the day, retailing is a very tough business, and people are very tired. We're open twenty-four hours a day now, but on Friday night when we used to close at eight o'clock or ten o'clock, I used to be in the store, and I used to stand at the back door with the manager and say to the manager, "Say thank you to the staff."

When I went round the stores—we had seven hundred or eight hundred by the time I left, so I couldn't go round them all in a year—I always used to write to the manager afterward and say, "Thank you very much;

great to see the store. You're doing a really very good job for us, and just thank everybody for the job they're doing."

So it's human touches—saying thank you and acknowledging people—that brings the spirit through for the company.

---

## TAKEAWAYS

⚏ The most important person in an organization should also be the most humble. Leaders should not assume they are "God's gift" to the field.

⚏ Leaders should never underestimate the power of personal visits to motivate people. Getting close to staff and managing them on a personal level can have a profound effect on their performance and attitudes.

## Leading by Example

❧ Leaders must remember to treat staff with respect—by acknowledging them on a daily, informal basis while also thanking them formally for the work they do.

———■◆◆◆■———

# A Leader
# Is Shaped by
# His Team

———■◆◆◆■———

## Warren Bennis

*Distinguished Professor of Business
Administration, Marshall School of Business,
University of Southern California*

I, LIKE MOST OTHER PEOPLE of my
generation, went into the army when I was
eighteen—I was three weeks away from being
eighteen—and actually enlisted. But it didn't

# Leading by Example

make any difference. There were 18 million people in uniform in 1943 when I joined the army.

I went to UCLA to become a sanitary engineer—which basically means digging bathrooms, latrines for the people in the front lines—and I was totally unsuited for engineering. Luckily, they ended the program, not because of my inadequacy or incompetence, but they had realized in 1940, roughly—this was in late 1943—that there was going to be a big [invasion] that was going to start in 1944, and they would need hundreds of thousands of men—mainly men; there were just a few women then—to open up the front in France and Germany. It was called D-Day.

So they ended the [sanitary engineering] program, and I volunteered for officer candidate school and went through four months of training at the Infantry School in Fort Benning, Georgia—what's sometimes called "Benning School for Boys." Four months of the best education I've ever had. Hard. I say that because if you evaluate edu-

# Leading by Example

cation in terms of preparing you for what you're going to do in the future, I've never had a better education than those four months in Fort Benning to prepare me for being a platoon leader in the infantry.

The interesting thing about becoming the "authority"—and notice, I'm using quotes around the word "authority"—I joined a company that had been in combat since D-Day, the 84th Infantry division— known as "the Railsplitters"—of the Illinois National Guard. It's the National Guard of Abraham Lincoln, a venerable infantry division with a great history. I joined as a replacement officer, Spec 15-42, which means that I joined a platoon of men who'd been in combat through very tough times, and they trained me to be their leader. Can you imagine that?

What I learned, then, was how powerful that band of brothers was for shaping me. I began getting very interested in the idea of the power of groups, the power of the bond. I think there may be brave people and, I want to be clear on this, I think there may be courageous people—that a certain quality is endowed in an individual, and it makes that person courageous. But I think most of what we call courage and bravery is a function of belonging to a group for which you will take a bullet for somebody else. I did not think and still don't think I am a brave or courageous person, but I think that my platoon made it possible.

This is really a profound aspect of leadership: the understanding that the power of really feeling the trust and camaraderie of a group, understanding what a group is, and being part of a group—being bonded—can allow people the license to be at their best.

# TAKEAWAYS

⊣ Formal education is an important step that has its place in training individuals to become leaders. However, just because a person has had formal training and is given the title of "leader" does not mean that that individual has absolute "authority."

⚔ Sometimes, learning to be a leader means being on the front lines. The group being led can shape and train its leader, if the leader allows that opportunity for growth.

⚔ Leaders should embrace the power of the group, which creates an environment of great trust and camaraderie among its members. This power of the group and the bond of its members encourage its members—both leaders and staff—to do their best.

—▪◂◆▸▪—

# The CEO Sets
# the Tone

—▪◂◆▸▪—

## Domenico De Sole

*Former President and CEO, Gucci Group*

IT IS TOTALLY CLEAR to me that any
company wanting to be successful must have
a very precise sense about its mission: Where
are we going? How are we getting from A to
B? Most importantly, the manager, de-
pending on his or her level, must set the
tone. I think that is critical.

## Leading by Example

Work these days is seen to be much more sophisticated, especially if you're talking about senior management or middle management. They have to first understand: What is the mission? What's the company trying to achieve? Where are the goals of the company? These goals must be very clear, simple, and—most important—understandable.

What I say to everybody is that the mission should be clear and repeated all the time. It is important for a CEO to keep repeating the same basic principle and make sure that everybody at every level of the organization shares the mission, shares the dream, and understands what needs to be done.

By the same token I am a true believer that the management sets the tone, starting with the CEO. It is very difficult to say to people that they have to save money, for example, if there is then a wasteful management style. That's just an example, but it is true for everything. I think it is hard to create a culture of hard work and responsibility if the CEO is not held responsible and there is no culture of hard work at the CEO level.

In 1994, at the very beginning of my time at Gucci, I went to Italy. The number-one priority—and I saw it immediately—was to get everybody in agreement about the mission and understanding internally what were we trying to do, then to start executing it properly.

I used to be there all the time; go in at the crack of dawn and be in very late every night, working on weekends, calling everybody at all times. Every time I said that something needed to be done, I kept following up and calling back and saying, "Is it done? Is it done?" I was very visible.

At the time I was living in Florence and was visiting all our suppliers throughout the area. So I had a very strong presence within the organization and made sure that everybody communicated with me.

At that time I also had more people reporting to me, and the company was smaller, but certainly the sense that things were going to change, and that things needed to be done, was very strong. Everybody saw me working full time.

The previous CEO had never gone to Asia, which is bizarre, considering how strong luxury companies are there. So I started traveling to Asia constantly. It was an important market for us to grow, so I established a very strong presence and showed a lot of people that there was very strong personal commitment on my part.

I really do feel that one of the important tenets for a CEO or a manager is to set the tone, be the leader, be the example, and make sure that everybody views you as the person who practices what he preaches, because this is important. Also, I think the mission has to be simple, clear, and repeated all the time to make sure that it filters through the entire organization, so everybody really understands the goal of the company, what it is trying to achieve, and how to get there.

## TAKEAWAYS

- The CEO must set the tone at the top of a company to ensure it is clear about its mission and how it will get there.

- Managers and other leaders must work tirelessly to encourage a hardworking culture throughout the organization, aligned to the same set of values.

- Leaders should be as visible as possible by regularly visiting all departments—whether they are in the same building or in different countries. They must not restrict themselves to headquarters.

—◆◆◆—

# If You're Going to Lead, Trust Your Judgment

—◆◆◆—

## Howard Lester

*Chairman and CEO, Williams-Sonoma*

WHEN THE INTERNET CRAZE started back in the 1990s, we were under intense pressure in our company to get Web sites out there and develop Web sites. I remember, we had a fellow from Goldman Sachs come out. He said, "[The Web is] going to be 40 percent of your business and three years of your revenues." This is the guru from Goldman. Different people who would do work for us would come and give us proposals, wanted us to get started and spend $50 million, or whatever it was. We had companies—very substantial companies—coming to us to do a joint venture and spin it out into a public entity.

And yet I couldn't understand how it was going to work, why there was going to be this flock of people going to our site on the Web. So I was reluctant to allow our company to invest seriously in the Internet when we had no plan or no idea at all of where we were going. I didn't have a vision for the Internet. I remember saying, "I feel like it's a train coming down the track, but I feel the train's a lot farther away than other people do." And I felt that we had time, because I believe so fervently in the power of brands.

As I thought about it, I thought, "It's going to be very difficult to develop a brand, a new brand, just because you're on the In-

# Leading by Example

ternet. You're going to have to advertise it
an incredible amount and spend a lot of
money doing it, and I just don't understand
the idea of starting a business and just
building the top line and incurring great
losses and not having a plan to get profitable; I just don't understand that." It was
against everything I'd learned in my whole
business career. So we stayed out of it.

Probably for three or four years after we
were strongly encouraged by everybody to
get into the Internet, we stayed out of it—
again, because we felt we had all the skills to
excel at [our business]. We had the catalogs
out there; we were branded with the cus-
tomer; we had the skills to display goods; we
knew how to photograph them to sell them
in a direct way; we knew how to write the
copy; we knew how to ship the goods; we had
the distribution center; we knew how to
pack [shipments]; we had the call centers;
we knew how to take care of the customers.
So we had all of the pieces, but we just
weren't ready. And so we waited, and fortu-
nately we were right.

## Leading by Example

It turned out that when we finally went on the Web, we started with a bridal registry site for our Williams-Sonoma brand, and that did well. We've now expanded our Web presence to all of our other brands, and I think last year it represented about a $600 million business for us. So we thought it through, and we made a profit from day one. Our return on our investment has been equal to or bigger than it was in the other channels, and it's been a very successful experience for us.

I guess the lesson I learned there—or reinforced the lesson that I already had learned—is, trust your own judgment. If you're going to lead, and you have a vision of where you're trying to go, it's not always an unchallenged vision, or you're not always going to be surrounded by yes people; you're going to be challenged in your vision, and you're going to be challenged in your decisions. And great leaders have a strength of conviction. You have a responsibility to really think through what you're doing. You ask a lot of opinions; it's not as if you go hide from everybody because you've made up your mind. But I think my point of view has always been if I have an opinion and people can't argue me out of it, then I must be right. And I have to have the strength of that conviction and the courage to stick to it.

# TAKEAWAYS

- ⚔ At different points in time, business leaders will face intense pressure to follow trends, especially when those trends lead to promises of increased revenues.

- ⚔ Without a clear vision or plan of action, leaders must proceed with caution. Even when a business has all of

## Leading by Example

the pieces to embark on a new venture,
it doesn't make sense to do so until the
venture can be proved profitable.

⊰ When leaders face extreme pressures to
proceed, they must remain steadfast,
trust their own judgment, and have the
courage to stick to it.

—————◆◆◆◆—————

# Having the Courage of Your Convictions

## Amelia Fawcett

*Former Vice Chairman and COO,*
*Morgan Stanley International*

—————◆◆◆◆—————

ANYBODY CAN MAKE an easy decision. I think what probably defines true managers are those who are able to make quite difficult choices.

# Leading by Example

I remember at the end of 1993, we'd had a record year at the firm. Our then chairman, Dick Fisher, decided that we needed to make a significant investment—particularly in head count—to make a quantum leap in market share for the firm. This was very much in sync with his oft-articulated strategy and view that the firm was globalizing fast, as were our clients, and in order to be successful we needed to be as strong in local markets as we were globally—and we were a little behind in some markets.

So the decree went out that people should look around and come back with suggestions on where they wanted to add head count, and where we were light on the ground and needed to invest to make a meaningful difference in that relevant market. The plans were approved, and everybody started hiring people. It was a particularly important time for Europe—where we were a bit underinvested—and I think a lot of the resources indeed came our way.

However, in 1994, there was the Mexican debt crisis, and the financial markets had a very major wobble. Many financial services firms were staring at potentially significantly reduced revenues and income, and started to pull back. And we looked to Dick and said, "Well, in this kind of environment, should we continue?" And he said, "No, our long-term strategy is right—continue." So we continued to hire, and then the markets got worse and most of our competitors started laying people off, and again people said, "Do you really want us to continue?" And he replied, "Absolutely; the strategic imperative is the same."

By the end of 1994, which was indeed a tough year, despite howls of protest from industry analysts—and a fair amount of skepticism within certain quarters of the firm—we had completed our plan and added 15 percent to our head count. That was a significant amount at the time. And in 1995 and 1996, we took very large amounts of market share in almost every major market—particularly the markets outside the United States.

Frankly, the foundation for the growth that we've had since then—particularly here in Europe—was clearly set in the investments that we made at that time.

I think Dick, and the courage of his convictions, were an inspiration to me and to many others at Morgan Stanley. It was a powerful example of why, in addition to short-term opportunities and focus on growth and profitability, you need to remember where you're going and what your long-term investment and strategic goals are. At the end of the day, despite difficulties in the market, if you still believe that the fundamental, strategic direction is correct, you have to have the courage of your convictions and stay the course, regardless of how unpopular people might think that decision is.

In 1994, we made a bet on Russia that if you were going to service and be important in the natural gas industry, you had to be able to understand it and be a player there. So we built an office and, in the midnineties, started to add more people. But in 1998, with the Russian debt crisis, it became clear that that was going to be a serious

# Leading by Example

problem and potentially a cost that many firms weren't willing to take.

But we still felt that, over the longer term, you could not be a player in the natural resources industry without understanding and being a part of the Russian scene. So unlike our competitors, we stayed the course. We trimmed the office down somewhat, and we put our growth plans on hold, but we kept the office there—we kept its people there and we maintained a focus on our clients there when most of our competitors closed their offices and fired their staff. That meant that we were able to maintain, and still have, a leading franchise; it's only recently that our competitors have returned.

Anyone can make decisions: we all make decisions every day, but so do the people who work for us. The real test is people who can make difficult decisions, who can stand up to unpopular decisions and criticism, and who have the courage of their convictions to do what they think is right and keep in mind the strategic long-term goal.

---

# TAKEAWAYS

---

⛩ By committing to a long-term strategy, leaders can bring significant competitive advantages for their businesses. They must not be tempted to give in due to short-term pressure or criticism: instead, they should stay focused and stay the course. They must make sure to articulate clearly what the vision is.

⛩ Leaders should not shy away from detractors to their endeavors. Conflict can unearth flaws in the plan. Instead, they should invite people to air their views at an open meeting, or privately, and answer each of their issues in turn.

# ⚔ ABOUT THE ⚔
## CONTRIBUTORS

**Sanjiv Ahuja** is the chief executive of Orange
Group.

Mr. Ahuja started his career at IBM in 1979 as
a software engineer and stayed there for fifteen
years, fulfilling various executive roles, the most
senior of which included the responsibility of
leading IBM's entry into the telecommunications
software industry.

He moved on to become president of Telcordia
Technologies (formerly Bellcore), the world's
largest provider of operations support systems, net-
work software, and consulting and engineering
services to the telecommunications industry. He
then became CEO of Comstellar Technologies, the
California-based technology company.

In April 2003 Mr. Ahuja joined Orange as
COO, moving up to CEO of the Group in March
2004, a position he holds today. He is also a director of Cadbury Schweppes.

**Dawn Airey** is the former managing director of Sky
Networks, a position she left in 2007 to become
CEO of Iostar.

# About the Contributors

Ms. Airey has worked in television for twenty years. She joined Britain's Central TV as a management trainee in 1985 and became Channel 4 liaison officer a year later. In 1988 she was made controller of program planning. The following year she became director of program planning, with specific responsibilities for the schedule and its off- and on-screen promotion. In January 1996 she was appointed director of programs for Channel 5 (now Five). She became CEO in October 2000—a position she held until the end of 2002. In January 2003 she joined British Sky Broadcasting, where she took on the newly created post of managing director, Sky Networks, until her departure 2007, when she joined the global communications company Iostar.

Ms. Airey is also a director of EasyJet.

**Warren Bennis** is University Professor and Distinguished Professor of Business Administration, and Founding Chairman of The Leadership Institute at the Marshall School of Business at the University of Southern California.

Professor Bennis has served on the faculty of MIT's Sloan School of Management, where he was chairman of the Organizational Studies Department. He is a former faculty member of Harvard and Boston University, and former provost and executive vice president of State University of New York at Buffalo. He was president of the University of Cincinnati from 1971 to 1977.

# About the Contributors

Professor Bennis is also chairman of the Advisory Board of the Center for Public Leadership at Harvard's Kennedy School. He has written more than two dozen books and many articles on leadership, change, and creative collaboration. He is a consultant for *Fortune* 500 companies and has served as adviser to four U.S. presidents.

**Julia Cleverdon** is the CEO of Business in the Community.

Ms. Cleverdon started her career working in industrial relations at British Leyland. She was director of The Industrial Society's Education and Inner City Division from 1981 until 1988 before becoming CEO of Business in the Community—the movement of seven hundred companies across the United Kingdom committed to continually improving their positive impact on society—in 1992.

During her time there, one of her key roles has been to lead "Seeing is Believing," the initiative launched in conjunction with HRH the Prince of Wales to help business leaders see the role business can play in tackling social problems. To date, more than fourteen hundred business leaders have taken part.

Ms. Cleverdon is also a director of InKind Direct, the charity that acts as a clearinghouse for surplus goods from the corporate sector that are channeled to good causes in the voluntary sector.

# About the Contributors

**Domenico De Sole** is the former president and CEO of Gucci Group. He is currently a director of Bausch & Lomb, Telecom Italia, Delta Air Lines, and Gap Inc.

Mr. De Sole moved from Italy to the United States in 1970, where he earned a master's degree from Harvard University and became a partner in the Washington law firm of Patton, Boggs & Blow. He joined Gucci in 1984 as CEO of Gucci America. He remained in New York until 1994, when he moved to Italy as the Group's chief operating officer.

He was appointed CEO, and at the end of 1995 led Gucci Group NV's listing on the New York and Amsterdam stock exchanges. In 1999 he successfully fought a hostile takeover bid, securing Gucci's independence as a basis for continued expansion, which has included the acquisition of Yves Saint Laurent, Alexander McQueen, and Stella McCartney. Mr. De Sole left Gucci in 2004.

**Amelia Fawcett** is the former vice chairman and COO of Morgan Stanley International. Ms. Fawcett is currently deputy chairman of the National Employment Panel.

She had been with Morgan Stanley for seventeen years, first joining the London office in 1987. She was then appointed vice president in 1990, and executive director in 1992, moving up to the role of managing director and chief administrative officer for the European operations in 1996.

# About the Contributors

In 2002 she was appointed vice chairman of Morgan Stanley International, responsible for development and implementation of the company's business strategy. She left her position in September 2006.

Ms. Fawcett is also chairman of the National Portrait Gallery's Development Board and chairman of the London International Festival of Theater.

**Ken Freeman** is the current managing director of the private equity firm KKR (Kohlberg Kravis Roberts & Co.) and the former chairman and CEO of Quest Diagnostics.

Mr. Freeman started his career at Corning Incorporated, progressing through the financial function to lead several business turnarounds. In 1996 Quest Diagnostics, the health-care services company, was spun off from Corning.

Following his nine-year tenure at Quest Diagnostics, Mr. Freeman joined KKR as its managing director in May 2005. In this role he works closely with KKR's health-care team and other industry groups to source new investment opportunities and provide operational counsel and management expertise.

**Howard Lester** is the chairman and CEO of Williams-Sonoma.

Mr. Lester purchased Williams-Sonoma in 1978, and since that time has held the positions of president, CEO, and now chairman.

# About the Contributors

Mr. Lester is also on the board of Harold's Stores and is on the executive council of UCSF. He is on the advisory boards of the Retail Management Institute of Santa Clara University and the Walter A. Haas School of Business at the University of California, Berkeley.

**Lord MacLaurin** is the former chairman and CEO of Tesco. He spent thirty-eight years at the international retailer Tesco, a company he joined in 1959 and subsequently expanded into a retailing tour de force. Currently, Lord MacLaurin is a director for The Evolution Group and a member of the Heineken Supervisory Board.

Lord MacLaurin was chairman of Tesco from 1985 until 1997, and prior to that had been CEO of the organization for twelve years. Lord MacLaurin was knighted in 1989, and given a life peerage in 1996.

He was also chairman and CEO of Vodafone, the global mobile phone operator, from June 2000 until July 2006. Although he is retired from the board, Lord MacLaurin continues to serve as an adviser to Vodafone.

**Sir David Michels** is the former group chief executive of Hilton Group, a position he left in 2006. Currently, he is the group chief executive for Scandic Hotels.

Sir David joined Ladbroke Group in 1981 as sales and marketing director of Ladbroke Hotels.

He then became managing director of Ladbroke's Leisure Division in 1983 and was named managing director of Ladbroke Hotels in 1985. Following Ladbroke Group's acquisition of Hilton International in 1987, Sir David became Hilton's senior vice president, sales and marketing. In 1989 he moved up to become deputy chairman of Hilton UK and executive vice president of Hilton International.

He joined Stakis as CEO in 1991. Eight years later the company was acquired by Hilton Group for around £1.2 billion. He joined Hilton International as CEO in April 1999 and became Group CEO of the Hilton Group (formerly Ladbroke Group) in June 2000. He left the company in 2006.

Sir David is also a director of British Land Company, EasyJet, Marks & Spencer, and Strategic Hotels & Resorts.

**William Pollard** is the chairman emeritus of the ServiceMaster Company.

Mr. Pollard joined ServiceMaster in 1977 and served his first term as CEO over the decade spanning 1983 until 1993. During that period the organization experienced a major change in its structure and direction, including the rapid growth of its Consumer Group.

In 1999 he returned as CEO, and remained in the role for sixteen months until his successor had been identified and elected. Mr. Pollard was also chairman of ServiceMaster from 1990 until April 2002, and remains an adviser to the company.

**Sir Michael Rake** is the current chairman of KPMG International.

Sir Michael joined KPMG (Peat Marwick) in 1972 and worked in Europe, where he ran the audit practice in Belgium and Luxembourg from 1984 to 1986, before moving to the Middle East to run the practice for three years.

After transferring to London in 1989, he became a member of the UK Board two years later and had a variety of leadership roles before being elected UK senior partner in 1998, then International chairman in 2002. He moved on to become chairman of KPMG in Europe and then Chairman of KPMG International and senior partner of KPMG in the United Kingdom. During his tenure he has overseen the campaign to ensure a progressive and pragmatic legislative response post-Enron.

**Lord Sharman** is currently chairman of the Aegis Group, a position he has held since 1999.

He joined Peat Marwick Mitchell (later KPMG) as a manager in 1966. He worked in a number of overseas offices before being appointed a partner in the London branch in 1981.

From 1987 he was responsible for the group's national marketing, and then three years later for operations in London and the South East. From 1991 to 1994 he was chairman of KPMG Management Consulting worldwide. In 1994 he was appointed a senior partner.

He also served as a member of the International Executive Committee and on the European Board. In 1997 he became chairman of KPMG International and retired from the company in September 1999.

Lord Sharman is also a director of Reed Elsevier, BG Group, Aviva, and Group 4 Securicor.

**Will Whitehorn** is the president of Virgin Galactic.

Mr. Whitehorn's early career included time as a helicopter crewman in the North Sea for British Airways. He was also a market intelligence officer for the TSB Group flotation and a graduate trainee with Thomas Cook Group.

Mr. Whitehorn joined Virgin Group in 1987 as head of corporate public relations. He became Virgin Group's brand development and corporate affairs director, in this role acting as Sir Richard Branson's spokesman.

He was also responsible for the corporate image of Virgin, public affairs, global brand development, selected company stewardship, and a number of new business development activities. In 2004 he was appointed president of Virgin Galactic. Virgin plans to launch its inaugural mission late in 2008.

## ⊰ ACKNOWLEDGMENTS ⊱

First and foremost, a heartfelt thanks goes to all of the executives who have shared their hard-earned experience and battle-tested insights for the Lessons Learned series.

Angelia Herrin, at Harvard Business School Publishing, consistently offered unwavering support, good humor, and counsel from the inception of this ambitious project.

Julia Ely, Hollis Heimbouch, and David Goehring provided invaluable editorial direction, perspective, and encouragement. Much appreciation goes to Jennifer Lynn for her research and diligent attention to detail. Many thanks to the entire HBSP team of designers, copy editors, and marketing professionals who helped bring this series to life.

Finally, thanks to our fellow cofounder James MacKinnon and the entire Fifty

# Acknowledgments

Lessons team for the tremendous amount of time, effort, and steadfast support they devoted to this project.

—Adam Sodowick
  Andy Hasoon
  Directors and Cofounders
  Fifty Lessons